The Wisdom of the Celts

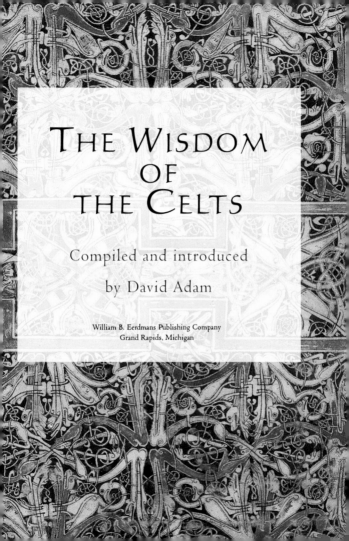

THE WISDOM OF THE CELTS

Compiled and introduced

by David Adam

William B. Eerdmans Publishing Company
Grand Rapids, Michigan

This edition published 1996 in the USA
through special arrangement with
Lion Publishing by
Wm. B. Eerdmans Publishing Co.
255 Jefferson Ave. S.E., Grand Rapids, Michigan 49503

Printed in Singapore

01 00 99 98 97 96   7 6 5 4 3 2 1

ISBN 0-8028-3833-2

CONTENTS

INTRODUCTION

The early Celts saw God's presence in all things.
Although there never was a Celtic church as
such, there is no doubt that the Celtic peoples
added a great richness to the Christian church.
They brought with them a strong enthusiasm for
life, a love of the world, a spirit of adventure and
a deep awareness of God in ordinary life. God
could be met with on the road and discovered in
his creation; God, creation and the human being
are interwoven in wonderful ways. This may be
hard to put into words but was often expressed
in Celtic art. Yet they did distinguish between
God and created things. They said all things
belonged to God and were contained in him, as
the greater contains the lesser.

Because God was the Maker of the
world, the world was seen as good. So they could
ask, 'How can one love God without loving his
creation?' Respect for God was shown in respect
for all around them. The Celts saw themselves as
part of creation and not separate from it, so

Columbanus could say, 'He who tramples on the earth tramples on himself.' The Celts realized that to harm the earth is to show contempt for its Creator, and it has been suggested that, if the Celtic understanding of our oneness with the world had survived, we would not be having our current ecological problems. They saw the world as the primary way God communicates with people. It is through creation that God reaches out to us and through creation we understand him. If we get our understanding of creation wrong, this affects our understanding of God. It is of little use being able to read books if we cannot 'read' the world around us.

Though the Celts believed the world was good, they believed it was  under enemy occupation. They were in no doubt that we could be attacked at any time by the power of evil. They were well aware of the dangers of living and of the corruption that besets society. So, many of their prayers were for protection, for strength to survive, for discernment between good and evil. They knew themselves as frail beings but at the same time given strength by the Almighty.

The early Celts were very much aware of the living presence of Jesus Christ in their lives and many of their prayers were directly to him. They also emphasized the threefold nature of God as Father, Son and Holy Spirit, and this gave a threefold pattern to many of their prayers of dedication

When speaking of the Celtic church, we usually mean the early Christians in Brittany, Cornwall, Ireland, Scotland and Wales. They were not separate from the rest of the church and their influence was felt throughout England and Europe. The predominance of Irish and Scottish prayers is only due to the good fortune of their survival when so much has been lost.

CREATION

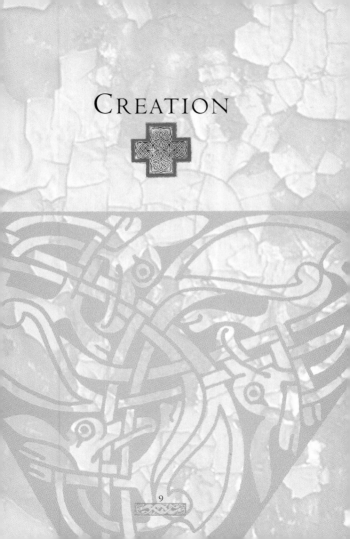

GOD OF ALL

Our God is the God of all,
The God of heaven and earth,
Of the sea and of the rivers;
The God of the sun and of the moon
and of all the stars;
The God of the lofty mountains
and of the lowly valleys
He has His dwelling around heaven and earth,
and sea, and all that in them is.

St Patrick

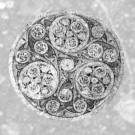

GOD IN ALL

He inspires all,
He gives life to all,
He dominates all,
He supports all.
He lights the light of the sun.
He furnishes the light of the night.
He has made springs in dry land.
He is the God of heaven and earth,
of sea and rivers,
of sun, moon and stars,
of the lofty mountain and the lowly valley,
the God above heaven,
and in heaven,
and under heaven.

St Patrick

ALMIGHTY CREATOR

Almighty Creator, it is you who have made
the land and the sea...

The world cannot comprehend in song
bright and melodious,
even though the grass and trees should sing,
all your wonders, O true Lord!

Old Welsh

GOD REVEALED IN CREATION

If you want to understand the Creator,
seek to understand created things.

Columbanus

MORNING PRAYER

I believe, O God of all gods,
That Thou art the eternal Father of life;
I believe, O God of all gods,
That Thou art the eternal Father of love.

I believe, O God of all gods,
That Thou art the eternal Father of the saints;
I believe, O God of all gods,
That Thou art the eternal Father of each one.

I believe, O God of all gods,
That Thou art the eternal Father of mankind;
I believe, O God of all gods,
That Thou art the eternal Father of the world.

From Carmina Gadelica

PROCLAIMING HIS GOODNESS

There is no life in the sea,
There is no creature in the river,
There is naught in the firmament,
But proclaims His goodness.
Jesu! Jesu! Jesu!
Jesu! meet it were to praise Him.

There is no bird on the wing,
There is no star in the sky,
There is nothing beneath the sun,
But proclaims His goodness.
Jesu! Jesu! Jesu!
Jesu! meet it were to praise Him.

From Carmina Gadelica

THE THREE EVERYWHERE

The Three who are over my head,
The Three who are under my tread,
The Three who are over me here,
The Three who are over me there,
The Three who are in the earth near,
The Three who are up in the air,
The Three who in heaven do dwell,
The Three in the great ocean swell,
Pervading Three, O be with me.

Poems of the Western Highlanders

GOD WITH US

CHRIST WITH US

My dearest Lord,
Be Thou a bright flame before me,
Be Thou a guiding star above me,
Be Thou a smooth path beneath me,
Be Thou a kindly shepherd behind me,
Today and evermore.

St Columba

THE PATH OF RIGHT

My walk this day with God,
My walk this day with Christ,
My walk this day with Spirit,
The Threefold all-kindly:
Ho! ho! ho! the Threefold all-kindly.

My shielding this day from ill,
My shielding this night from harm,
Ho! Ho! both my soul and my body,
Be by Father, by Son, by Holy Spirit:
By Father, by Son, by Holy Spirit.

Be the Father shielding me,
Be the Son shielding me,
Be the Spirit shielding me,
As Three and as One:
Ho! ho! ho! as Three and as One.

From Carmina Gadelica

THE PATH I WALK

The path I walk, Christ walks it.
May the land in which I am in
be without sorrow.
May the Trinity protect me wherever I stay,
Father, Son and Holy Spirit.
Bright angels walk with me
dear presence—in every dealing...

May every path before me be smooth,
man, woman and child welcome me.

Attributed to St Columba
from Celtic Christian Spirituality

11

PRAISING GOD

Let us praise God
at the beginning
and the end of time.
Who ever seeks Him out
He will not deny
nor refuse.

From Black Book of Carmarthen

FAITH AND WORKS

The tempests howl, the storms dismay,
But manly strength can win the day.
Heave, lads, and let the echoes ring.

For clouds and squalls will soon pass on,
And victory lie with work well done.
Heave, lads, and let the echoes ring.

The king of virtues vowed a prize
For him who wins, for him who tries.
Think, lads, of Christ and echo him.

From Columbanus In His Own Words

DEDICATION

DEDICATION

Rule this heart of mine,
O dread God of the elements,
That Thou mayest be my love,
that I may do Thy will.

From Selections from Ancient Irish Poetry

FOR LIGHT

Lord grant me,
I pray Thee in the name of
Jesus Christ the Son,
my God,
that love which knows no fall
so that my lamp may feel thy kindling touch
and know no quenching;
may burn for me
and for others may give light.

Prayer of Columbanus

BE THOU MY VISION

Be Thou my Vision, O Lord of my heart:
Naught is all else to me, save that Thou art,
Thou my best thought, by day and by night,
Waking or sleeping, Thy presence my light.

Be Thou my Wisdom, Thou my true Word,
I ever with Thee, Thou with me Lord.
Thou my great Father, I Thy dear son
Thou in me dwelling, I with Thee one.

Ancient Irish

GOD'S PATH

'Tis God's will I would do,
My own will I would rein;
Would give to God his due,
From my own due refrain;
God's path I would pursue,
My own path would disdain.

From Poems of the Western Highlanders

PROTECTION

THE PROTECTION OF CHRIST

Christ as a light
Illumine and guide me!
Christ as a shield overshadow and cover me!
Christ be under me! Christ be over me!
Christ be beside me,
On left hand and right!
Christ be before me, behind me, about me!
Christ, this day, be within and without me!

St Patrick

THE SMOORING OF THE FIRE

The sacred Three
To save,
To shield,
To surround
The hearth,
The house,
The household,
This eve,
This night,
Oh! this eve,
This night,
And every night,
Each single night.
Amen.

From Carmina Gadelica

JESU MACMARY

Jesu MacMary, at dawn-tide, the flowing,
Jesu MacMary, at ebb-tide, the going:
When our first breath awakes,
Life's day when darkness takes,
Merciful God of all, mercy bestowing,
With us and for us be,
Merciful Deity,
Amen, eternally.

From Poems of the Western Highlanders

PROTECTION

May God shield me,
May God fill me,
May God keep me,
May God watch me.

May God bring me
To the land of peace,
To the country of the King,
To the peace of eternity.

From Carmina Gadelica

Journeying Blessing

Bless to me, O God,
The earth beneath my foot,
Bless to me, O God,
The path whereon I go;
Bless to me, O God,
The thing of my desire;
Thou Evermore of evermore,
Bless Thou to me my rest.

Bless to me the thing
Whereon is set my mind,
Bless to me the thing
Whereon is set my love;
Bless to me the thing
Whereon is set my hope,
O Thou King of kings,
Bless Thou to me mine eye!

From Carmina Gadelica

CONFIDENCE IN GOD

Alone with none but Thee, my God,
I journey on my way.
What need I fear, when Thou art near
O King of night and day?
More safe I am within Thy hand
Than if a host did round me stand.

St Columba

THE PROTECTING GOD

Lord be with us this day,
Within us to purify us;
Above us to draw us up;
Beneath us to sustain us;
Before us to lead us;
Behind us to restrain us;
Around us to protect us.

St Patrick

THE POWER OF GOD

May the strength of God pilot us,
May the power of God preserve us,
May the wisdom of God instruct us,
May the hand of God protect us,
May the way of God direct us,
May the shield of God defend us,
May the host of God guard us
against snares of evil
and the temptations of the world.

St Patrick

GOD IN OTHERS

CHRIST IN OTHERS

Christ the lowly and meek,
Christ the all-powerful,
Be in the heart of each to whom I speak,
In the mouth of each who speaks to me,
In all who draw near me,
Or see me, or hear me!

St Patrick

THE GIFT

I am the Gift, I am the Poor,
I am the Man of this night.

I am the Son of God in the door,
On Monday seeking the gifts.

From Carmina Gadelica

BLESSING OF THE KINDLING

I will kindle my fire this morning
In presence of the holy angels of heaven,
In prsence of Ariel of the loveliest form,
In presence of Uriel of the myriad charms,
Without malice, without jealousy, without envy,
Without fear, without terror of any one under the sun,
But the Holy Son of God to shield me.
Without malice, without jealousy, without envy,
Without fear, without terror of any one under the sun,
But the Holy Son of God to shield me.

God, kindle Thou in my heart within
A flame of love to my neighbour,
To my foe, to my friend, to my kindred all,
To the brave, to the knave, to the thrall,
O Son of the loveliest Mary,
From the lowliest thing that liveth,
To the Name that is highest of all.
O Son of the loveliest Mary,
From the lowliest thing that liveth,
To the Name that is highest of all.

From Carmina Gadelica

HOSPITALITY

O King of the stars!
Whether my house be dark or bright,
Never shall it be closed to any one,
Lest Christ close His house against me.

If there be a guest in your house
And you conceal aught from him
'Tis not the guest that will be without it,
But Jesus, Mary's Son.

From Selections from Ancient Irish Poetry

PEACE

Peace between neighbours,
Peace between kindred,
Peace between lovers,
In the love of the King of life.

Peace between person and person,
Peace between wife and husband,
Peace between woman and children,
The peace of Christ above all peace.

From Carmina Gadelica

As You Did It To The Least Of These...

Remember the poor when you look out
on fields you own,
on your plump cows grazing.
Remember the poor when you look into your barn
at the abundance of your harvest.
Remember the poor when the wind howls
and the rain falls,
as you sit warm in your dry house...
The poor have no food except what you feed them
no shelter except your house
when you welcome them,
no warmth except your glowing fire.

From Celtic Fire

DOXOLOGY

As it was, as it is, and as it shall be
Evermore, God of grace, God in Trinity!
With the ebb, with the flow, ever it is so,
God of grace, O Trinity,
with the ebb and flow.

Poems of the Western Highlanders

Text Acknowledgments

Constable, from *Selections from Ancient Irish Poetry*, Kuno Meyer, 1928: pages 24, 43.

Taken from *Celtic Fire* by Robert van de Weyer, published and copyright 1990 by Darton, Longman and Todd Ltd (UK) and Bantam Doubleday Dell Publishing Group Inc. (US) and used by permission of the publishers: page 45.

Scottish Academic Press, from *Carmina Gadelica*, Alexander Carmichael, 1928: pages 14, 15, 19, 31, 33, 34, 41, 42, 44.

SPCK, from *Celtic Christian Spirituality*, Oliver Davies and Fiona Bowie, 1995: pages 12, 20. Used by permission of the publishers.

from *Poems of the Western Highlanders*, G.R.D. Maclean, 1961: pages 16, 27, 32, 47.

First published by Veritas Publications, from *Columbanus in his Own Words*, Tomas O' Fiaich, 1974: page 22. Used with permission.

Picture Acknowledgments

1: Royal Irish Academy/Phaidon Press Ltd; 2/3 Lichfield Cathedral Library;
4: The Board of Trinity College Dublin;
7 and 36: BL 36006 Add 39943 f.51 King Siegfried visits St Cuthbert and entreats him to accept the bishopric of Lindisfarne, by Bede, Latin (Durham), Life and Miracles of St Cuthbert (12th century) British Library, London/Bridgeman Art Library, London;
8, 32 and cover: BL 36008 Add 39943 f.2b St Cuthbert and two of the brethren returning from the land of the Picts by Bede, Latin (Durham) Life and Miracles of St Cuthbert (12th century) British Library, London/Bridgeman Art Library, London;
10, cover: The Board of Trinity College Dublin;
13: K103310 by permission of the British Library, London; 18: © 1996 The Trustees of the National Museums of Scotland;
24: LAM58195 Ms 1370 f.115v St Luke with crozier and book, Irish (Armagh) Macdurnan Gospels (9th century) Lambeth Palace Library, London/Bridgeman Art Library, London; 27, 30 and 45: The Board of Trinity College Dublin;
40: K2476 by permission of the British Library, London;
46: The Board of Trinity College Dublin